I0004717

Computer Building Made Simple
How to Build Your Own Computer

Revised Edition

by

Francis J. Ernissee

ISBN: 978-1-257-98505-0

* * * * *

PUBLISHED BY:

Francis J. Ernissee

Computer Building Made Simple:

License Notes

* * * * *

Introduction

You search the stores...You check online..And there it is...

That's the perfect computer for me. And look..it's only

$899.00.

"It's a great deal" you say.

What if I told you it was "not" a good deal at all.

That you could buy that computer for *50% less* or pay the same price and get twice the computer you're looking at?

People shop at Best Buy, Frys, CompUSA and other stores and pay the retail price for there computers and are very happy.

What they don't know has just cost them 40-50% more then they would have paid to

Build the Computer Yourself.

But I can't build my own computer! They are too complicated...it's rocket science, right?

I hear that all the time. Everyone that I have built computers for says;

"I'm the smartest person they have ever met".

I must be a genius or something! Helps to pad my ego, but the truth is I'm just an average guy. No smarter then you.

The difference is I can cook...

I can follow a recipe.

What!!

What the heck does cooking have to do with building a computer??

Let me ask you this...Can you follow a recipe? Not some complicated one, just a simple recipe?

If you answered "yes", then what you are about to read will save you hundreds of dollars and turn you into the *"smartest person your friends and family has ever met"*...

lol..still makes me laugh.

Hey! Lets get real!! It's complicated.."There is no way I could do this" Lets find out..

Take the test....

I'm going to show you a simple recipe. Then modify it to computer terms, just to let you know that it is not rocket science at all, but nothing more then knowing the *ingredients* and the *steps to follow* to get the desired product.

Whether it be cookies or computers, it's all in following the recipe.

Here is a cookie recipe from ALL recipes for;

Ultimate Chocolate Chip Cookies

Ingredients

3/4 stick CRISCO® Butter Flavor All-Vegetable
Shortening Sticks*
1 1/4 cups firmly packed light brown sugar
2 tablespoons milk
1 tablespoon vanilla extract
1 large egg
1 3/4 cups Pillsbury BEST® All Purpose Flour
1 teaspoon salt
3/4 teaspoon baking soda
1 (6 ounce) package semi-sweet chocolate chips
1 cup coarsely chopped pecans (optional)

Directions

1. Heat oven to 375 degrees F.
2. Combine shortening, brown sugar, milk and
   vanilla in large bowl. Beat at medium speed of
   electric mixer until well blended. Beat in egg.
   Combine flour, salt and baking soda. Mix into
   shortening mixture until just blended. Stir in
   chocolate chips and nuts.

3. Drop by rounded measuring tablespoonfuls 3 inches apart onto ungreased baking sheet.
4. Bake 8 to 10 minutes for chewy cookies, or 11 to 13 minutes for crisp cookies. Cool 2 minutes on baking sheet on a cooling rack. Remove cookies to rack to cool completely.
5. TIP* If nuts are omitted, add an additional 1/2 cup semi-sweet chocolate chips.

Look at the ingredients and the instructions..fairly simple right?

Now...lets see the same recipe in computer terms..

Custom Gaming Computer Core i7, GTX 580, 1TB, 8GB Mem

Blu-Ray DVD Burner, 850W PS
(as shown on eBay)

Ingredients

Case
Power Supply
Motherboard
CPU w/fan
Memory
Hard Drive
DVD Player
Video Card

Extra Cooling Fans (optional)
Software

Why Look!! There were ten ingredients to the cookie recipe and ten to the computer recipe...what a coincidence...

Instructions

Open the case
Install the power supply.
Install the motherboard
Install the CPU with Fan
Install the Memory
Install the Hard drive
Install the DVD Player
Install the Video Card
Install the optional cooling Fans
Install the Software

To be honest..this looks easier than the cookie recipe...and guess what?

It is!!

That is one of the computers I sell on eBay. And there is no cooking involved...

The only difference between you and I is that I know the **ingredients**.

That is what this book is all about...

I will explain each part of your computer...how to match them up...where to buy them and how to install them.

It's not rocket science at all...just simple steps and knowing the terms computer builders use.

When your done with my book, you will not only save yourself a lot of money, but you will be able to sell your very own computers on eBay and make money.

(The computer shown above sells on eBay for $1979.00. It cost less the $1400.00 to build. That's over $500.00 profit.)

You could skip my book and buy the computer at the store,

or...

Build it Yourself and save money.

It's up to you...

But I'm guessing that building your own computer sounds like fun and you want to be ;

"The smartest person your friends and family has ever known"

You will...

Never again pay the retail price for a computer!

Build computers and sell them online!

Repair your friends and family computers!

OK!

You made a great decision. You purchased the book. You want to build your own computers.

Now What?

First a little advice...

Remember the cookie recipe? There were certain "ingredients" and "steps" that needed to be followed to end up with "cookies". Each step had to be followed in order. Step two can not be done before step one, and three can not be done before step two and so on.

The same rule applies to building a computer. Check and be sure you have all the components or "ingredients". Focus on each installation step in order, and don't look at the next until you complete it.

When learning something new it is easy to become confused and make mistakes if you're looking ahead and not staying focused.

I suggest that you read the entire book first, then start building your computer.

By following the instructions in this book the total build time with software should be about three to four hours.

My Computer-What is all that stuff?

We're going to take a walk through a computer. If you already own one, shut it down, open it up and lets' see what's inside.

Each component will be introduced to you with an in depth description later in the book.

First, you need to see how few "ingredients" there are.

SO LETS' GET STARTED

Chapter One

THE BASICS

A Look Inside;

The box is called the "Case" or "Tower". A look inside seems a bit confusing at first. There are all sorts or wires and goodies..

Most of the wires are from the "Power Supply" and attach to the Motherboard, Optical Drives, Hard Drives and Fans. If you have a high end video card it may need power also.

There are a few that come from the front panel for USB ports, audio, reset, power on/off and the front panel lights.

That large printed circuit board is called the "Motherboard". Everything except the case cooling fans attach to the motherboard. There are the "Heat-sink, (under it is the Central Processing Unit or "CPU"), the "Memory Slots" and the "PCI Slots"

The Heat-sink on today's' computers also has a fan attached for better cooling of the CPU

The memory slots are for your system "Ram". Depending on what motherboard you use there may be two to four slots.

The "PCI" slots are for your video, audio, networking and other cards you may chose. A further discussion of these PCI cards will be later in the book.

To the upper right are the optical drive bays. These house the "DVD or CDROM" drives. These open in the front of your computer for ease of access to load software, play movies or copy things to disks.

Below that are the "Hard Drive" bays. All your files and programs are stored on your hard drive.

As you can see, there are not many components inside a computer, sort of like the ingredients in a cookie recipe. Your computer is made up of;

- Case-Tower

- Power Supply

- Motherboard

- CPU with heat-sink and fan

- Memory or RAM

- Hard Drive

- DVD or CD drive

- Video Card (optional)

- Software

- and a few misc parts(described later)

All of the above are termed as your system "Hardware"

Now we can describe each component in detail.

Note: All of the following picture are for reference purposes only and not necessarily the components you will use. They were taken from computers that I have build, or from the public domain on the internet.

Later in the book I will make a few suggestions as to what you should use.

The Tower

The computer tower protects and cools all of the hardware inside. It should be strong enough to take a hit without damage.

The most important aspect of the tower is "Cooling". Every component inside produces heat and must be cooled to run smoothly and not fail. Proper cooling is a must with today's computers. Chose a tower with a minimum of three or four fans...Also, the better the tower the easier it is to install all the hardware. You don't need the best tower on the market, but don't buy the cheapest either. When choosing a tower be sure it will house an full "ATX" board. Some suggestions will be given later in the book.

Keep in mind that the tower is also an expression of who you are, so pick something that makes you feel good and will impress your friends. Add that "WOW, you built that?".

When looking for a case, check the "Form Factor". Be sure it is ATX Mid-Tower or Full Tower.

Power Supply

This supplies power to the other components, which is why it has so many wires coming out of it.

It is usually positioned at the back top corner or the back lower corner of the computer case. The power supply has a fan built into it to keep itself and the computer cool.

The PS above is an 850 watt total output. Power Supplies come in a range from 480w-1200w. The higher the wattage the less chance of burning out your PS. So, get a good one, between 750w-1200w.

I like to use "Modular" power supplies. "Why", because the only cables hardwired to the unit are the motherboard power cables, the rest are plugged into the PS as needed. This cuts down on the amount of wires inside the case and makes for a neater installation. Also, the length of the cables are longer, eliminating extensions to short cables.

The price is a bit higher, but installing modular is much more efficient.

When ordering your PS, be sure it comes with two 6pin connectors for your video card. Most high end video cards have two power connections on them to run the card. You can always order extra cables as needed.

Suggestions on power supplies will be later in the book.

The Motherboard

The motherboard is the "heart" of the computer. It is the largest and most fundamental component of a PC and every other component is attached to it in some way.

This is because all the different components use the motherboard to communicate and work with each other.

The motherboard has a series of slots, sockets and connectors for attaching the components of a PC. In most cases, the memory, accessory cards, and CPU are installed directly onto the motherboard. The drives and peripherals communicate with the motherboard through wired connections.

There are a wide range of motherboards to choose from. They differ in features, speed, capacity and the CPU supported. They also differ in size, shape and layout, this is commonly referred to as the "form factor"

The above picture is of a 'Micro ATX". It has limited RAM slots and PCI slots. If your planning on expanding your system, this will cause problems. But, if eight gig of ram and one video card is all you need...this will do.

This is a full ATX. It has four RAM slots and supports two video cards, plus additional PCI cards. Plenty of expansion.

The CPU and Heat-sink/Fan

CPU stands for Central Processing Unit. This is the brain of the computer and is often referred to as the "processor" or the "chip". It is found under a heat sink and fan and sits directly on the motherboard.

The CPU directs, coordinates and communicates with the other components and performs all of the "thinking". It's not really thinking, what a CPU actually does is perform mathematical calculations.

It is the software that people write that translates those calculations into useful functions for us.

Documentation

Heatsink / Fan

Intel BX8060515760
Core i5 760 Processor

RAM /Memory

RAM stands for Random Access Memory, and comes as modules in predefined amounts. It is also found directly on the motherboard and usually in one, two or four slots. The memory chips store information, temporarily, for short term use by the CPU. RAM is used to store information for files that are actually being used by the CPU at any given time.

Documentation

Patriot PXD38G1600LLK Viper Xtreme Performance Desktop Memory Kit

The computer's RAM memory is an entirely different thing from the hard disk "memory". The hard disk stores information "permanently" for long term use.

The Hard Drive

A hard disk - which is also called a "hard drive" - is much like a filing cabinet. The programs and data are stored on the hard disk and the computer accesses them as they are needed. When the computer accesses the hard drive, it is reading and moving the stored information into the RAM memory. That memory is the temporary workspace. However, the original file is still on the hard disk and is left undisturbed until the file is saved.

When the computer stores or "saves" information, it writes the data to the hard disk. That process results in the old file being replaced or modified with the new information. If you save data to a new file, or install new software, the information is written to the disk in an available, unused portion of the disk.

DVD or CD Drive (optical drive)

The optical drive is often called a DVD drive, or a CD drive. It sits at the front of the computer for ease of access, and uses a laser to read and write information to CD's and DVD's.

It also is used to load software, play music and movies.

Today's DVD drives come in standard and Blu-Ray.

Video Card or Graphics Adapter

The graphics card or video card translates information into the graphics and text that appear on the monitor screen.

Modern motherboards have special PCI slots called PCI Express slots for your graphics cards.

Some have one slot while others have two so you can bridge both cards together for Extreme gaming. This is only an option and all games will run well on one card, provided it is of high quality.

Modern graphics adapters usually incorporate some memory right on the card to improve their performance.

Software- Your Operating System (OS)

Your OS will more than likely be Windows 7, but which one, that's up to you. If you are not going to use more that 4gb of ram, then install any 32bit version.

If you plan on expanding the system to say, 8gb or 16gb of ram you will have to install a 64bit version.

When you purchase Windows 7, there are two disks, one 32bit and one 64bit. Install which ever one you wish. They both work the same.

Other software that you will need will be an Anti-Virus and Firewall. Other than that, use your own discretion as to what you want on your computer.

Other PCI Cards

Audio cards, Network Interface Cards (NIC) and other PCI cards can be installed in the remaining pci slots. Most cards are Plug and Play, which means that Windows will load the drivers for the card when you turn your computer on.

Well, that's it...not as much in there as you may have thought. If you focus on each component, and install them per the instructions in this book, you will have your new computer up and running in no time.

As for your Monitor, Keyboard, Mouse, Speakers and other peripheral devices...well, that is up to you. I will say this, purchase good ones, you'll never regret it.

A few suggestions...Your monitor should be no smaller than 20". If your adding speakers, get a 2.1 system at least. It has a sub woofer that adds a surround sound aspect to your music or videos.

Your keyboard and mouse should be something that feels comfortable.

And just think...Never again will you have to pay retail to build or repair your computer.

Now that you are familiar with your computers hardware in simple terms, it's time to put together a shopping list. Pay close attention to your "ingredients". They need to match up to build your computer.

A complete order list of components will be provided for different systems after this chapter.

Chapter Two

Computers You Can Build

We are now going to look at several different computer systems. Each one complete for its' purpose.

The question to keep in mind is, "What will my computer be used for". You could build a computer for "Mom and Pop", to search the internet, get email or watch simple videos'. This is the least expensive machine and will suffice for the casual user.

On the other end of the spectrum is the "Gaming Computer". Those who want performance when playing graphic intensive games. Many of today's' games, such as World of Warcraft and Rift, also know as MMORPG games, require much faster machines, more ram and a high end video card.

With that said, I will give you a look at different systems and what they will be used for and provide a complete list of components.

Keep in mind that there is a very large selection to the design of a computer. As you learn more about yours, you will also see how to build different machines than those presented here.

Computer One (Low Range)

The following is an inexpensive computer. The cost without a video card is approx.$250. You can add a low end video card such as; Nvidia GeForce 8400gs for about $30. After adding your monitor, keyboard, Mouse and speakers for about $150, it makes this one a great computer for under $450 dollars.

ASUS P5G41-M LE/CSM Motherboard and Intel Pentium Dual-Core E6500 Processor and Corsair 2048MB PC6400 DDR2 800MHz Memory and Seagate Barracuda 1TB Low Power Hard Drive and Lite-On Internal 24X.

What in the world is all that?

When you go shopping on the internet this is some of what you will see.

This is called a "Barebones Bundle". Everything you need to build this computer is included in the bundle except for the Monitor, Keyboard, Mouse and Speakers. You can buy the components separately and get a different case for example or smaller hard drive, but if your satisfied with the look, this is a good start.

CD Not included

This computer is great for surfing the internet, checking e-mail, using Office, Facebook, Tweeter, You Tube and such. It does not include a graphics card, but use's the on board graphics from the motherboard. You can install a PCI-e video card and improve its' performance to play games at minimum settings.

Computer 2 (Mid Range)

Asus M4A79XTD EVO Phenom II X4 Barebones Kit - Asus M4A79XTD EVO Mobo, AMD Phenom II X4 965 CPU, Corsair 4GB DDR3 RAM, Seagate 1TB HDD, Ultra X-Blaster Mid Tower

Case, Ultra LSP550 550W Power Supply, XFX HD685XZNFC
Radeon HD 6850 Video Card.

The above computer is a decent Gaming Computer. It's fast and provides very good graphics support. This may be all you need to run your games at ultra settings.

The cost is around $650.00-$700.00 with Monitor, Keyboard, Mouse and Speakers.

Computer 3 (The Ultimate)

The following is a "Scream Machine". This is as good as it gets for the price. Add a 24" HD monitor, Keyboard, Mouse and some good speakers and your at $2000.00.

EVGA X58 FTW3 Core i7 Barebones Kit - EVGA X58 FTW3 Mobo, Intel Core i7-960 CPU, Corsair 12GB (3x 4GB) DDR3 RAM, Seagate 1TB HDD, 24x DVDRW, CoolerMaster HAF 932 Tower Case, Ultra LSP750 750-Watt PSU, EVGA 015-P3-1582-AR GeForce GTX 580 SuperClocked Video Card - 1536MB GDDR5, PCI-Express 2.0, Dual DVI, Mini HDMI, SLI, DirectX 11.

Just a few suggestions...if your going to spend this much money, change out the following;

Power Supply...up this to 1000 watts.

DVD...get a BluRay burner.

Sound...Bose

These suggestions will add about $500.00 to the price, but will be well worth it.

Chapter Three

What and Where to Buy

Places where I shop;

Tigerdirect.com

Tiger has great pricing and a very large selection. They ship fast, and if you plan on buying more than once, get there free shipping plan.

Geeks.com

You will find some very good deals at geeks. Many of there items are factory refurbished. The parts are of good quality, but may carry a limited warranty, so watch what you buy. Shipping is good and they have a good return policy.

Ebay

Buying from ebay requires knowing who your buying from. You can find some great deals, but be sure your dealing with a reputable seller. Check there rating first.

Frys'

If you have a Frys' in your town, this is a good place to get parts in a hurry. Look for the special discounts. Sometimes there pricing is lower than anywhere, even the net. I always check them out first for prices and some good ideas.

Now you have seen three systems. This should give you some idea of what you want to build for yourself or to sell online. Putting together a computer means matching up the components.

The following charts should provide you with many ideas. These are component match-ups that I use.

"Motherboards".

When choosing a motherboard there are three important things to know.

Form Factor; This is the size of the board, and will determine how much expansion is available. A "Micro ATX" is 9.6x9.6, length and width(24.4cm x 24.4cm). ATX is 12x9.6, length and width(30.5cm x 24.4cm).

CPU Supported; Generally, you decide which cpu you want to use before you get the motherboard. The cpu will determine the speed of your computer. The better your cpu..the faster your computer will be.

There are two manufactures of cpu's...Intel and AMD. If price is an issue, AMD will be the one for you. Intel though is faster and there is a wider selection.

Memory; This part is fairly easy. You have a choice between DDR2 and DDR3. Anywhere from 667MHz to 2200MHz overclocked. Choose the memory speed by matching it with the cpu's front side bus speed. If the cpu will support 1066MHz DDR2, then purchase accordingly.

When buying memory, stick with the name brands..Kingston, Corsair, Crucial, PNY and Patriot. These memory sticks are what keeps the processor from over working and helps set the speed for your computer. Buying cheap memory is never recommended.

The following will give you some ideas of what to purchase.

These are used as examples only.

There are many Manufactures and a variety of choices, but this is a good start.

Towers

Azza CSAZ-1000 Solano

Cooler Master Storm Scout

Cooler Master SGC-1000-KWN1 Storm Enforcer

NZXT gaurdian

NZXT Guardian 921

NZXT lexa_s

NZXT lexa

NZXT m59

NZXT PHAN-002GR Phantom

NZXT Tempest EVO Enthusias

NZXT vulcan

NZXT vulcan2

Thermaltake element G

Thermaltake VL90001W2Z Armor A90 Black

Thermaltake VL200K1W2Z Element V Black Edition Full Tower

Motherboards

When choosing a motherboard there are three important things to know.

1- Form Factor; This is the size of the board, and will determine how much expansion is available. A "Micro ATX" is 9.6x9.6, length and width(24.4cm x 24.4cm). ATX is 12x9.6, length and width(30.5cm x 24.4cm).

2- CPU Supported; Generally, you decide which cpu you want to use before you get the motherboard. The cpu will determine the speed of your computer. The better your cpu..the faster your computer will be.

There are two manufactures of cpu's...Intel and AMD. If price is an issue, AMD will be the one for you. Intel though is faster and there is a wider selection.

3- Memory; This part is fairly easy. You have a choice between DDR2 and DDR3. Anywhere from 667MHz to 2200MHz overclocked. Choose the memory speed by matching it with the cpu's front side bus speed. If the cpu will support 1066MHz DDR2, then purchase accordingly.

When buying memory, stick with the name brands..Kingston, Corsair, Crucial, PNY and Patriot. These memory sticks are what keeps the processor from over working and helps set the speed for your computer. Buying cheap memory is never recommended.

The following will give you some ideas of what to purchase.

These are used as examples only.

There are many Manufactures and a variety of choices, but this is a good start.

Motherboards

Socket 775 (Intel)

"ASUS P5G41-M LE"

Micro ATX

Intel Core 2 Duo

Intel Core 2 Extreme

Intel Core 2 Quad

667MHz DDR2

800MHz DDR2

1066MHz DDR2

"MSI G41M-P25"

Micro ATX

Intel Core 2 Duo

Intel Core 2 Quad

800MHz DDR3

1066MHz DDR3

1333MHz DDR3

"ASUS P8H67-M LE"

Micro ATX

2nd generation Intel® Core™ i3

2nd generation Intel® Core™ i5

2nd generation Intel® Core™ i7

Non-ECC Unbuffered memory

DDR3 1333MHz

DDR3 1066MHz

"ASUS P8P67 Pro"

ATX

2nd generation Intel® Core™ i3

2nd generation Intel® Core™ i5

2nd generation Intel® Core™ i7

DDR3 1333MHz

DDR3 1066MHz

DDR3 1600MHz

DDR3 1866MHz (OC)

DDR3 2133MHz (OC)

DDR3 2200MHz (OC)

Socket 1366 (Intel)

"ASUS SABERTOOTH X58 "

ATX

Intel Core i7

Intel Core i7 Extreme

1066MHz DDR3

1333MHz DDR3

1600MHz DDR3

1866MHz DDR3

"ASUS Rampage II"

ATX

Intel Core i7

Intel Core i7 Extreme

1066MHz DDR3

1333MHz DDR3

1600MHz DDR3 (OverClocking)

1800MHz DDR3 (OverClocking)

2000MHz DDR3 (OverClocking)

2133MHz DDR3 (OverClocking)

2200MHz DDR3 (OverClocking)

Socket AM2+ (AMD)

"Asus M2N68-AM PLUS"

Micro ATX

AMD Athlon

AMD Sempron

AMD Phenom

AMD Phenom II

AMD Athlon II
667MHz DDR2
800MHz DDR2
1066MHz DDR2

"Asus M4A785-M"

Micro ATX
AMD Athlon
AMD Sempron
AMD Phenom
AMD Phenom II
AMD Athlon II
667MHz DDR2
800MHz DDR2
1066MHz DDR2
1200MHz DDR2 (OverClocking)

Socket AM3 (AMD)

"Asus M4N75TD"

ATX
AMD Sempron
AMD Phenom II
AMD Athlon II
1066MHz DDR3
1333MHz DDR3
2200MHz DDR3

"ASUS CROSSHAIR IV Formula"

ATX
AMD Sempron

AMD Phenom II

AMD Athlon II

1066MHz DDR3

1333MHz DDR3

2200MHz DDR3 1866MHz DDR3 (OverClocking)

Socket AM3+ (AMD)

"ASUS Sabertooth 990FX"

ATX

AMD Phenom II

AMD Athlon II

Sempron 100 Series

DDR3 1333MHz

DDR3 1066MHz

DDR3 1600MHz

DDR3 1866MHz

"ASUS Crosshair V Formula"

ATX

AMD Phenom II

AMD Athlon II

AMD Sempron 100 Series

AMD FX

DDR3 1333MHz

DDR3 1066MHz

DDR3 1600MHz

DDR3 2000MHz (OC)

DDR3 1800MHz (OC)

CPU's. (Central Processing Unit)

As mentioned earlier, choosing a CPU will determine what Motherboard you will need, so first ask the questions...

"What will this computer be used for".

"Will I want to expand its' use"

There are two manufactures of CPUs', Intel and AMD. Each can do the job.

Intel provides a wider selection, and is a bit pricier. While AMD is lower in cost, you may find that it is all you need.

CPUs' are compared against each other by benchmarking. This is simply showing how the cpu performed running different programs. A stress test is used to see were the cpu will begin to falter. The numbers can be a bit confusing, but they do provide a good comparison between them.

The following list will give you and idea of where each cpu stands by comparison, and the approximate price of that cpu.

The following chart is courtesy of PassMark.com

Processor	PassMark CPU Mark Score	Price (USD)
Intel Core i7 980X @ 3.33GHz	10,607	$1,108.40*
Intel Core i7-2600K @ 3.40GHz	9,782	$314.99*
Intel Core i7-2600 @ 3.40GHz	8,899	$299.99*

Intel Core i5-2500K @ 3.30GHz	7,241	$214.99*
Intel Core i7 960 @ 3.20GHz	6,670	$284.99*
Intel Core i7 950 @ 3.07GHz	6,359	
Intel Core i7-2630QM @ 2.00GHz	6,294	NA
Intel Core i7 870 @ 2.93GHz	6,071	$289.90*
AMD Phenom II X6 1090T	6,052	$179.99*
Intel Core i7 930 @ 2.80GHz	5,836	$341.99*
Intel Core i7 920 @ 2.67GHz	5,564	$279.99*
Intel Core i7 860 @ 2.80GHz	5,563	$395.06*
AMD Phenom II X6 1055T	5,189	$154.99*
Intel Core2 Quad Q9650 @ 3.00GHz	4,621	$339.99*
Intel Core i5 760 @ 2.80GHz	4,559	$197.99*
Intel Core2 Quad Q9550 @ 2.83GHz	4,372	$289.99*
AMD Phenom II X4 965	4,282	$134.99*
Intel Core i5 750 @ 2.67GHz	4,266	$214.99*
Intel Core2 Quad Q9450 @ 2.66GHz	4,040	$398.95**
AMD Phenom II X4 955	3,955	$119.99*
Intel Core2 Quad Q9400 @ 2.66GHz	3,817	$212.22*
Intel Core2 Quad Q8400 @ 2.66GHz	3,683	$181.99*
AMD Phenom II X4 940	3,681	$104.99**
AMD Phenom II X4 945	3,622	$109.99*
Intel Core2 Quad Q9300 @ 2.50GHz	3,586	$226.99*
Intel Core i7 740QM @ 1.73GHz	3,565	$407.53*
Intel Core2 Quad Q8300 @ 2.50GHz	3,553	$162.99*

AMD Athlon II X4 640	3,468	$99.99*
Intel Core i7 720QM @ 1.60GHz	3,275	NA
Intel Core2 Quad Q8200 @ 2.33GHz	3,268	$229.95*
AMD Athlon II X4 630	3,253	$79.99*
Intel Core i5 650 @ 3.20GHz	3,147	$179.99*
AMD Phenom 9950 Quad-Core	3,063	$156.99**
AMD Athlon II X4 620	2,983	$89.00**
Intel Core2 Quad Q6600 @ 2.40GHz	2,981	$398.95*
AMD Phenom 9850 Quad-Core	2,963	$108.00*
Intel Core i3 530 @ 2.93GHz	2,726	$130.95*
Intel Core i5 460M @ 2.53GHz	2,606	NA
Intel Core i5 450M @ 2.40GHz	2,465	NA
Intel Core2 Duo E8500 @ 3.16GHz	2,416	$204.08*
Intel Core i5 520M @ 2.40GHz	2,359	$326.52**
Intel Core i5 430M @ 2.27GHz	2,358	$79.00**
AMD Phenom 9500 Quad-Core	2,297	$89.96**
Intel Core2 Duo E8400 @ 3.00GHz	2,250	$178.99*
Intel Core i3 370M @ 2.40GHz	2,219	NA
Intel Core i3 350M @ 2.27GHz	2,048	NA
Intel Core2 Duo E7500 @ 2.93GHz	2,013	$108.09*
Intel Core i3 330M @ 2.13GHz	1,963	NA
Intel Core2 Duo E6850 @ 3.00GHz	1,922	$123.00*
Intel Core2 Duo E7400 @ 2.80GHz	1,918	$161.99**
AMD Phenom II X2 550	1,887	$84.99**
Intel Core2 Duo P8700 @ 2.53GHz	1,792	$285.50*

Intel Core2 Duo T9400 @ 2.53GHz	1,761	$354.94**
Pentium Dual-Core E5300 @ 2.60GHz	1,732	$115.60*
AMD Athlon II X2 250	1,713	$59.99*
Intel Core2 Duo T9300 @ 2.50GHz	1,710	$307.00*
Intel Core2 Duo E6750 @ 2.66GHz	1,687	$119.50*
Pentium Dual-Core E5200 @ 2.50GHz	1,665	$77.26**
AMD Athlon 64 X2 Dual Core 6000+	1,646	$198.95*
Intel Core2 Duo P8600 @ 2.40GHz	1,620	$227.73*
AMD Athlon 7750 Dual-Core	1,568	$70.00**
Intel Core2 Duo T6600 @ 2.20GHz	1,553	NA
Intel Core2 Duo P8400 @ 2.26GHz	1,551	$197.79**
AMD Athlon 64 X2 Dual Core 5600+	1,541	$101.00**
Intel Core2 Duo T8300 @ 2.40GHz	1,536	$236.00*
Intel Core2 Duo E6600 @ 2.40GHz	1,508	$339.95**
Intel Core2 Duo E6550 @ 2.33GHz	1,455	$93.50*
AMD Athlon 64 X2 Dual Core 5200+	1,423	$45.39**
AMD Athlon 64 X2 Dual Core 5000+	1,361	$195.02*
Intel Core2 Duo T6400 @ 2.00GHz	1,339	$72.79**
AMD Athlon 64 X2 Dual Core 4800+	1,313	$60.00*
Intel Core2 Duo E4500 @ 2.20GHz	1,274	$110.00*
Intel Core2 Duo T7500 @ 2.20GHz	1,273	$167.39**
Intel Core2 Duo E6400 @ 2.13GHz	1,272	$298.95*
AMD Athlon 64 X2 Dual Core 4600+	1,265	$210.00**
Intel Pentium Dual E2200 @ 2.20GHz	1,244	$91.99**

AMD Athlon 64 X2 Dual Core 4400+	1,194	$298.95**
AMD Athlon 64 X2 Dual Core 4200+	1,156	NA
Intel Core2 Duo T7300 @ 2.00GHz	1,151	NA
Intel Core2 Duo T7200 @ 2.00GHz	1,147	$498.95**
Intel Pentium Dual E2180 @ 2.00GHz	1,127	$179.95**
Intel Core2 Duo E6300 @ 1.86GHz	1,115	$157.00*
Intel Core2 Duo T7250 @ 2.00GHz	1,100	$257.56*
AMD Athlon 64 X2 Dual Core 3800+	1,047	NA
Intel Pentium D 3.40GHz	931	NA
Intel Core2 Duo T5500 @ 1.66GHz	922	$197.00**
Intel Pentium D 3.00GHz	813	NA
Intel Pentium D 2.80GHz	742	NA
AMD Athlon 64 3500+	567	$55.99*
Intel Pentium 4 3.40GHz	550	NA
AMD Athlon 64 3200+	530	$139.95**
Intel Pentium 4 3.20GHz	524	NA
Intel Pentium 4 3.00GHz	491	NA
AMD Athlon 64 3000+	491	$34.79*
Intel Pentium 4 3.06GHz	473	NA
Intel Pentium M 1.73GHz	448	NA
Intel Pentium 4 2.80GHz	416	NA
Intel Pentium 4 2.66GHz	336	NA
Intel Pentium 4 2.40GHz	314	NA
Intel Atom N270 @ 1.60GHz	304	

Lets examine the chart to show you what to shop for.

First, I'm going to start with the cpu that I use...the same one that is processing this book. If you look up the chart you will see it highlighted...Intel Core2Duo E6600. It received a score of 1,508. So what does this tell me?

First, let me tell you that I also play games on this computer, World of Warcraft , which is a MMORPG game with intense graphics. I use a Nvidia8800gt video card and have the settings in the game on medium. I run 4GB of DDR2 ram and have had no problems.

So a score of 1500 or above will allow you to play games, not a gaming machine, because I can't set the in game settings to ultra, but you get the idea.

Anything above the score of 1500 will be a better cpu for what I do on my computer. As you can see, there are a lot of cpus' to choose from. So price becomes important. There is no reason to pay a high price. Just because it's more expensive, doesn't make it a better CPU. When you combine a decent CPU with a good graphics card your PC's performance is greatly enhanced.

So what is a good passmark number...Low range=up to 2500...Mid range=2500 to 3999....High range=4000+.

Choose the CPU and Graphics card together. A good Graphics card will run $150.00+.

Also, the prices you see are "retail". Most of the time with a little searching you will find a better price....so shop around.

Memory
RAM=Random Access Memory

Ram is what the CPU uses to run programs and applications. As the cpu processes information, it stores the needed data in memory for easy access. The data in memory is constantly changing depending on what the cpu needs at that moment, therefore, ram is very fast.

Ram comes in sticks that attach to the motherboard in special slots next to the cpu. The amount of ram that can be installed is dependent upon your operating system and the number of slots on the motherboard.

Windows 7 for example, comes in two venues...32bit and 64bit. The difference between the two is in there processing, not there appearance.

A 32bit OS will only use up to 4GB's of ram. If your intent is to expand beyond that, then you should install a 64bit version, and you'll be able to install up to 32GB's.

Whatever you decide, RAM is very important. 4GB's will be enough for just about any application on the market today, but soon it will be the minimum requirement, so it may be wise to consider a 64bit OS. This will allow for future expansion.

There are many manufactures of memory. There are also different types of memory. We are not going to discuss the many different types because we are building PC's, so we will we will focus on DDR2 and DDR3.

But of even more importance is the Manufacturer. Not all ddr2 and ddr3 is the same. Quality is important. Your cpu will love you for installing a good quality ram.

Most computers sold today are using DDR3...Simply put, it is an upgraded version of DDR2.

The main choice that you have is "Who makes it".

Crucial, Kingston, G-Skill, PNY and Corsair are the top of the line. Stick with one of those and you can't go wrong.

Graphic Cards

If your going to build a low end computer you can skip this part, but by now your probably already thinking mid range, so lets get into the importance of Video Cards.

When looking on the store shelf you will see many video cards. They come in fancy boxes and tell you how great they will perform in your computer. So, how do you choose?.

Just as with CPUs', graphic cards are bench marked to measure there performance. The following chart will give you an idea of what to get and what it may cost. Remember, always shop around. These prices are retail and it is very likely you will find a much better price.

The following chart is courtesy of PassMark.com

Video card	PassMark G3D Score	Price (USD)
GeForce GTX 580	3,862	476.64*
GeForce GTX 570	3,562	319.99*
GeForce GTX 480	3,530	299.99*
GeForce GTX 560 Ti	2,966	224.99*
GeForce GTX 470	2,963	199.99*
Radeon HD 6870	2,842	189.99*
Radeon HD 6850	2,837	159.99*
Radeon HD 5870	2,717	749.99**
Radeon HD 5850	2,502	234.99**
GeForce GTX 460	2,355	159.99*
GeForce GTX 285	2,064	179.99**
GeForce GTX 280	1,962	NA

Radeon HD 4890	1,938	NA
GeForce GTX 275	1,911	NA
Radeon HD 4870	1,744	NA
GeForce GTX 260	1,739	99.99**
GeForce GTX 295	1,713	289.99*
Radeon HD 5770	1,664	129.99*
Radeon HD 4870 X2	1,539	NA
Radeon HD 5750	1,497	114.99*
GeForce GTS 450	1,440	99.99*
Radeon HD 4850	1,334	89.99**
Radeon HD 4770	1,263	NA
Radeon HD 4830	1,254	59.99**
Radeon HD 5670	1,244	69.99*
GeForce 9800 GTX+	1,116	NA
GeForce 9800 GTX/9800 GTX+	1,096	NA
GeForce GTS 250	1,070	99.99*
GeForce 8800 GTX	1,048	NA
GeForce 8800 GTS 512	1,010	NA
GeForce 9800 GX2	975	NA
Radeon HD 3870	967	NA
GeForce 8800 GT	966	NA
GeForce 9600 GT	930	139.99**

GeForce 9800 GT	914	114.99*
GeForce 8800 GTS	861	NA
Radeon X1950 Pro	823	NA
Radeon HD 3850	801	NA
GeForce GT 240	772	54.99*
Radeon HD 4670	762	49.99*
Radeon HD 5570	761	54.99*
Mobility Radeon HD 5730	719	NA
GeForce 7950 GT	665	112.95*
Mobility Radeon HD 5650	627	NA
GeForce 7900 GS	608	NA
GeForce 9600 GSO	580	69.99**
GeForce 8600 GTS	521	NA
Mobility Radeon HD 4650	521	NA
Radeon HD 4650	463	46.99*
GeForce GT 220	450	49.99**
GeForce 7600 GT	395	83.95*
GeForce 8600 GT	386	NA
Radeon HD 2600 XT	379	NA
Intel HD Family	371	NA
GeForce 9500 GT	352	51.99*
GeForce 9600M GT	335	NA
Intel	333	NA

Media Accelerat or HD		
Intel HD	326	NA
Radeon HD 5450	314	39.99*
Radeon HD 3670	302	NA
Mobility Radeon HD 4570	286	NA
GeForce 8600M GT	286	NA
GeForce 9400 GT	274	74.99*
Radeon HD 2600 PRO	264	NA
GeForce 6600 GT	249	64.95**
GeForce 8500 GT	237	NA
GeForce 7600 GS	236	NA
GeForce 7300 GT	230	NA
Radeon HD 4350	229	34.99*
GeForce 8600M GS	210	NA
GeForce 210	203	33.30*
Intel G41 Express Chipset	180	NA
Intel G33/G31 Express	165	NA
Radeon HD 4250	158	NA
GeForce 9300M GS	154	NA
Mobility Radeon X1400	147	NA
GeForce 6600	146	NA
Radeon HD 3450	144	31.99*

Radeon HD 4200	141	NA
GeForce 8400 GS	139	29.99*
GeForce 8400M GS	124	32.95*
Intel 82945G Express	117	NA
Mobile Intel 945GM Express	117	NA
Intel 82915G/G V/910GL Express	116	NA
Radeon HD 3200	106	NA
Mobile Intel 915GM/G MS 910GML Express Chipset F	88	NA
Mobile Intel 965 Express	87	NA
Mobile Intel 945 Express	81	NA
GeForce 7300 LE	77	NA
GeForce 7300 GS	77	NA
GeForce 8200M G	77	NA
Intel Media Accelerat or 3150	74	NA
GeForce 6200	57	39.99*
Intel 82865G Controller	57	NA
GeForce 7025 / nForce 630a	57	NA
GeForce	52	NA

6150SE nForce 430		
GeForce FX 5200	45	**29.99***
GeForce 6150 LE	45	**NA**
Intel 82852/828 55. GM/GME Controller	44	**NA**
Intel 82845G/G L/GE/PE/. GV Controller	31	**NA**

So...What do these numbers mean?

You remember that I use a Nvidia 8800gt card. It is highlighted and has a score of 966.

This card is a low end video card.

Below 1000=Low End

1000 to 2000=Mid Range

Above 2000=High End

As you can see there are many choices with a wide price range. Choosing a mid range or above video card will greatly enhance your PC's performance.

Not all of the prices were available but can easily be found on the net.

Remember to shop around for the best price.

The Other Components

The five most important parts of your new computer have been discussed. Now lets take a quick look at what is remaining.

Power Supply

Low end...480W minimum.

High end...850W minimum.

Hard Drive

The prices on today's hard drives are relatively the same between a 500gb and 1tb drive. So purchase what you believe you will need. Get a brand name and be sure the disk speed is at least 7200rpm. Also, purchase a SATA drive, not an IDE.

DVD R/W

This is a mater of choice. You can go with an inexpensive player or a very good Blu-Ray.

Only get a Blu-Ray player if you intend to watch HD movies on your computer that you rent or buy.

Movies and videos' that you watch on the internet are handled by your video card.

Audio Card

Almost all of today's motherboards have surround sound audio built onto the board, so this is an optional card.

If your going to add a great speaker set, I would recommend installing a audio card. A Sound Blaster would be a good choice.

Misc Parts

Fans, Fans, Fans...All of the towers shown earlier allow for 4 or 5 fans. It is recommended that you install as many as the tower will hold. Keeping the components cool is very important.

Another thing to consider is noise. When purchasing your fans get the ball bearing drive. These are very quiet.

Software

Windows 7 is what is out now. It comes in 32 and 64 bit. Both discs are in the box when you purchase it.

Low end computers with 4gb or less memory should use the 32bit version.

If your planning on installing more than 4gb of memory, load the 64bit version.

The home version of Windows 7 will suffice in most situations.

Most internet providers offer a free Security Suite. This contains a Firewall and Anti Virus program. If yours does not, purchase one like McAfee, Nortons, Bit Defender, Panda. Etc;

This will protect your computer from outside intrusion.

That about raps it up for the parts your will need. Now lets put the machine together.

Chapter Four

Installation Steps

Remember the cookie recipe? Well...now it time to get baking and build your new computer.

As with the cookies, you'll need to follow the proper steps. Look for the instructions that come with your tower for where the bays are located for different devices.

Be sure you have all the parts and tools to do the job.

The only tools you will need are a phillips head screwdriver with a magnetic tip and needle nose pliers.

Step 1...

Install all of your Fans.

Step 2...

Install your Power Supply.

Step 3...

Install your Hard Drive and DVD Player.

Step 4...

Install the CPU and Fan/Heat-sync onto the Motherboard. The instructions for proper installation comes with the Motherboard and CPU.

Step 5...

Install the Memory onto the motherboard.

Step 6...

Install the Motherboard into the tower.

Step 7...

Follow the instructions that come with the Motherboard to connect the Power cables and front panel device cables to the board.

Now connect your power cables and SATA cables to your Hard Drive and DVD Player. Use SATA 1 on the motherboard for your hard drive and SATA 2 for your DVD.

Connect your fans to the power supply. You may need a few 6pin splitters to give you extra connections to the supply.

Step 8...

Install your Video Card. If you are using a medium to high end card, you will find a 6pin power connection at the end of the card. Be sure this is connected if present.

Step 9...

Install the remainder of your PCI cards if you have them.

Attach your Monitor, Keyboard, Mouse, and Internet connection to the motherboard using the connections on the back of your computer.

Be sure the Monitor is attached to your Video Card (if your using one), the rest of your devices will be using USB ports.

Your speakers will attach to the USB ports or the sound connections on the motherboard under the USB ports unless you installed an Audio Card. Then attach them to this card.

Step 10...

Plug your Monitor and Power Supply and power for your speakers into a power strip with surge protection.

Turn on your computer.(Flip the switch on the power supply and press the button in the front of the computer).

Step 11...

Place your Windows 7 disc into the DVD player and Reboot your computer.

Follow the instructions for installing the Operating System.

If all of the components are working properly you will now have a working machine.

CONGRADULATIONS...

You have just built your first computer.

Now install your security suite and whatever other software programs you desire and go brag to your friends and family. You just accomplished something most of them can not do.

BUT WAIT!!

My computer did not come on...

NOW WHAT DO I DO??

Trouble Shooting

Don't get frustrated if this happens. Even the best technicians have this occur on a daily basis.

Even though all components are tested before leaving the factory, sometimes they are DOA (Dead on Arrival).

What you need to do now is find out which component is causing the problem.

Bad Power Supply (PSU) – How to Check If a Power Supply is Dead

My Computer Won't Turn On... Is My Power Supply Faulty?

Troubleshooting a Bad Power Supply is pretty straight forward. Since the Power Supply is self contained issues with the PSU are not usually the result of a configuration issue.

There are several you can check though before deciding the power supply is faulty. The first and foremost method is to use a power supply tester to check for a faulty PSU. Unfortunately not people own one until they need one, so there are some manual troubleshooting steps you can perform to check for a bad power supply.

How To Troubleshoot a Bad or Faulty Power Supply (PSU)

- WARNING: Power Supplies contain internal components that can store an electrical charge. Never attempt to repair the internal components of a Power Supply as you risk personal injury and also void the warranty on the PSU.

01. Check that the AC Power Cable is Connected Firmly to the Wall Outlet and PSU.

The PSU can commonly be stiff when connecting the AC power cable so make sure the cable and power supply are making good contact with one another.

02. Check the AC Outlet that the Power Supply is Plugged Into.

If it is a wall outlet, ask yourself if it is controlled by a wall switch. If so is the switch turned on?

If you are using a power strip or surge protector check to make sure the power switch is set to "On". There will usually be a little red light that indicates this on a decent power strip or surge protector.

03. Check the On/Off switch on the Power Supply itself.

Most new power supplies all have an On/Off switch. This is a little black switch on the back of the power supply that has a one and a zero on it. (It may look like an I / O on the switch).

Make sure this switch is set to "On". If the switch is set to one (1) this indicates that the power supply is turned "On". If it is set to zero (0) it means the PSU is currently switched off. Make sure the switch is set to the one (1) position.

04. Check the Voltage Switch on the Power Supply.

On most new Power Supplies there is a red switch on the back that indicates voltage. This can be set to either 115V or 230V.

In the USA all our households use 115V from the wall AC outlets for standard appliances. If you are in the US make sure your Power Supply is set to 115V. If you are from Europe I believe your PSU needs to be set to 230V.

05. Check the 20/24 Pin ATX Power Connector and 4 Pin ATX Power Connector

Most motherboards require that you connect two Power Leads from a Power Supply to power your motherboard.

The main power lead is the 20/24 Pin ATX power connection which plugs in near the memory slots on your motherboard. The secondary power lead that is required is the 4 pin ATX power connection.

Make sure both of these leads are plugged in securely to your motherboard. You should feel a small click when they are properly inserted.

It is not uncommon for a lead to feel stiff and not go in all the way. To ensure that the ATX power leads are firmly connected disconnect each on and reconnect them to the motherboard.

06. Use Observations on the Power Supply to Determine if it's Faulty.

- If your motherboard has a power LED on it, is this light turned on. (The motherboard power LED will normally glow even when the system is powered down.) If it is glowing this confirms the board is receiving power from the PSU and the problem may lie elsewhere.
- Can you see or hear the fan inside the power supply spin when you try to power on the system. If you do not see or hear it spinning this can be a sign of a bad power supply.
- Did the power supply make any crackling or popping noises when you tried to start the system? If so, this is a sign that a component inside the power supply has failed.
- Did you see a spark or smoke come out of the power supply? If so this is another sign that a component inside the Power Supply has failed.
- Does the power supply smell like burning electrical components. If so this is another sign of component failure inside the power supply.

07. Use Another Power Supply for Testing

If you have performed all of the above steps and have still not been able to determine if your issues are a result of a bad power supply use an extra power supply (if applicable) or a PSU from another system and try to start your system with the secondary Power Supply.

If it powers on with the other power supply you have determined your original Power Supply is bad or faulty.

Troubleshooting a Bad Power Supply Summary

If you have determined your Power Supply is bad you have two main options.

- If your power supply is under warranty send it into the retailer or manufacturer for RMA replacement.
- If your power supply is outside of the warranty period you will need to purchase a new power supply.

If the power supply is working but your computer won't start then follow this guide.

Pull the memory, video card and any other pci cards and try starting.

If it starts you will need to install each memory card and PCI card, one at a time and restart.

When it fails, replace that memory module or PCI card.

If it does not start with the memory and pci cards out, then disconnect the power and SATA cables from the DVD and Hard Drive.

Does it start?

If yes then power off and plug in all cards and the DVD player...if it starts you have a bad Hard Drive, if it does not then you have a bad DVD player.

If you would like further information on PC troubleshooting try

http://www.ehow.com/computers/

Conclusion

Now you have built your first computer, and it probably won't be your last.

You have bragging rights and the possibility of opening up your own computer business on eBay.

The sky is the limit.

The following are a few links to places that may interest you.

Places where I shop;

Tigerdirect.com

Tiger has great pricing and a very large selection. They ship fast, and if you plan on buying more than once, get there free shipping plan.

Geeks.com

You will find some very good deals at geeks. Many of there items are factory refurbished. The parts are of good quality, but may carry a limited warranty, so watch what you buy. Shipping is good and they have a good return policy.

Ebay

Buying from ebay requires knowing who your buying from. You can find some great deals, but be sure your dealing with a reputable seller. Check there rating first.

Frys'

If you have a Frys' in your town, this is a good place to get parts in a hurry. Look for the special discounts. Sometimes there pricing is lower than anywhere, even the net. I always check them out first for prices and some good ideas.

Ebay Guides

As was mentioned at the start, once you learn how to build your own computers, there is a great opportunity to start your own business,

Selling your creations on eBay is very easy, and the extra income comes in handy.

Below are a few links to help you get started;

http://pages.ebay.com/sellerinformation/howtosell/sellingbasics.html

http://ebay-selling-guide.blogspot.com/

http://netforbeginners.about.com/cs/buyingselling/a/eBay101.html

http://www.momscape.com/articles/selling-on-ebay.htm

http://www.fadedgiant.net/html/ebay_selling_tips_.htm

I hope this book suites your purpose. And even if you don't get to build your own computer, the cookie recipe is really good...you need to try them.